Fidel Castro
CUBA: AGAINST TERRORISM AND AGAINST WAR

Speeches on September 11; 22; 29 and October 6, 2001
Statements and documents

EDITORA POLÍTICA/ Havana, 2001

Translation: *ESTI*
Edition: *Iraida Aguirrechu* and *José Quesada*
Design: *Alejandro Greenidge Clark* and *Emilio Gómez*
Composition: *ESTI* and *Abel Cobo*

© On this edition:
Editora Política publisher, 2001

All rights reserved. No part of this work may by reproduced in any way without the authorization of the the publisher.

ISBN 959-01-0487-8 (Spanish)
ISBN 959-01-0488-6

Editora Política
Fax: (537) 556896 / 556836
Email: editora@epol.cipcc.inf.cu
edit63@ip.etecsa.cu
Belascoaín No. 864, Ciudad de La Habana

EDITORIAL NOTE

Humanity is living through a critical moment in history. War, with the destruction and death it always brings, is the chosen response to the terrorist attacks against the North American people committed last September 11th. International law, national sovereignty and the authority of the United Nations are also under threat.

CUBA: AGAINST TERRORISM AND AGAINST THE WAR *is the synthesis of our country's principled position, publicly expressed by president Fidel Castro ever since the 11th when, in the name of every Cuban citizen, he expressed our solidarity with the North American people in the face of such a brutal act and expressed our disposition to offer whatever medical assistance we could, within the limits of our resources and possibilities.*

These positions have been elucidated and explained by Fidel Castro before national and international public opinion in the revolutionary open forums held in San Antonio de los Baños, in Ciego de Ávila and in the Plaza de la Revolución "José Martí". The latter coincided with the 25th anniversary of the shocking terrorist act committed against a Cubana de Aviación plane which blew up in mid-air, killing all 73 passengers and crew. The positions adopted before these grave problems have been supported by the more than 1.5 million people attending the forums.

The National Assembly of Popular Power, in an extraordinary session in honor of the Barbados martyrs, agreed to adhere to existing international instruments against terrorism and condemned the bellicose policies and coercion used in international relations.

This book includes the texts of the four speeches of president Fidel Castro and the declarations of the Cuban government, creating the awareness that the terrorist plague cannot be fought with war, but rather with international action, coordinated by the United Nations.

SPEECH THE DAY OF THE TRAGIC EVENTS THAT OCCURRED IN THE UNITED STATES

(Fragments)

City of Havana, september 11, 2001

Teachers, construction workers, workers, students, relatives and guests:

We will see how this goes because ceremonies in stadiums, and similar places like this coliseum, are always complicated since part of the audience are behind you, some are on one side, some are on the other, and when somebody calls out, "I can't hear you," then the problems begin. [*Applause and shouts.*]

Yesterday [*Shouts of: "We can't hear you over here!"*]... All right, then I will leave and talk to you on TV. [*Shouts of "No!"*] Make a bit of an effort. You over there, who seem to be having the hardest time, have some patience and help us to maintain order here today. [*Shouts of: "You can hear it, you can feel it, Fidel is here."*]

As I was saying, yesterday was a quiet day, we were getting ready for two important events. First, the reopening of the school and the enormously important course that was beginning with this group of students. And also, many of our compatriots were waiting for news on the results of the famous Grammy awards, where a large and important delegation of Cuban artists was participating.

When we headed home in the wee hours of morning, quite late, our only worry was whether or not it would rain at the school, since there had been heavy showers on the previous days, and almost always at around the time the ceremony was scheduled. Just in case, we took the precaution of setting up an alternative venue for the inauguration of the course and the reopening of the school.

We planned ahead, and it is a good thing we did, because with all the rain that fell today, the place where we were going to hold the ceremony would have been flooded and muddy, even though a special place had been set up for the ceremony, where about 12,000 people were to take part, including students, relatives, guests, workers and community people.

Well, we had only been resting for a short time when the news started coming in about the dramatic events taking place in the United States. That news was and is of great importance. We immediately adopted the measure of asking the Cuban television network to broadcast information on what was happening there, with rigorously factual reports, even using footage from U.S. television broadcasts. Then we had to wait to see what would happen. Additionally, it was a very cloudy and rainy day here.

We did not even consider postponing the ceremony. It could not be postponed, despite the international tension created by such events. I would imagine that almost everyone knows about them, but to briefly summarize, at approximately 9:00 this morning, a Boeing airplane, a really big one, crashed straight into one of the two New York famous towers which make up one of the highest buildings in the world. Naturally, the tower caught on fire because of all the fuel from such a big airplane, and some horrific scenes began. And then, 18 minutes later, another plane, also from an U.S. airline, crashed straight into the second tower.

At the same time, a few minutes later, another plane crashed into the Pentagon. News arrived, in the midst of a certain amount of confusion, of a bomb outside the State Department, and other alarming events, although I have mentioned the most important.

Obviously, the country had fallen victim to a violent surprise attack, unexpected, unimaginable, something truly unheard of. And the scenes that ensued were appalling, especially when the two towers were burning, and foremost when they both collapsed, all 100 floors, spilling over onto neighboring buildings, when it was known that there were tens of thousands of people working there, in offices representing many companies from various countries.

It was only logical that this would be a shock for the United States and the rest of the world. The stock markets started to collapse, and because of the political, economic and technological importance and the power of the United States, the whole world was shaken up today by those events. So, we had to follow the events throughout the day, but at the same time, we also had to continue thinking about the conditions and circumstances in which this ceremony would take place.

Therefore, there were two issues: the school and the extremely important course it will offer, and the political and human catastrophe that had taken place over there, especially in New York.

[…]

Today is a day of tragedy for the United States. You know very well that hatred against the American people has never been sown here. Perhaps, precisely because of its culture, its lack of prejudice, its sense of full freedom —with a homeland and without a master— Cuba is the country where Americans are treated with the greatest respect. We have never preached any kind of national hatred, or anything similar to fanaticism, and that is the reason for our strength, because our conduct is based on principles and ideas. We treat all Americans who visit us with great respect, and they have noticed this and said so themselves.

Furthermore, we cannot forget the American people who put an end to the Vietnam War with their overwhelming opposition to that genocidal war. We cannot forget the American people who —in numbers that exceeded 80% of the population— supported the return of Elián González to his homeland. We cannot forget their idealism, although it is often undermined by deception, because —as we have said often times— in order to mislead Americans to support an unjust cause, or an unjust war, they must first be deceived. The classic method used by that huge country in international politics is that of deceiving the people first, to count on their support later. When it is the other way around, and the people realize that something is unjust, then based on their traditional idealism they oppose what they have been supporting. Often these are extremely unjust causes, which they had supported convinced that they were doing the right thing.

Therefore, although unaware of the exact number of victims but seeing those moving scenes of suffering, we have felt profound grief and sadness for the American people.

We do not go around flattering any government, or asking for forgiveness or favors. We neither harbor in our hearts a single atom of fear. The history of our Revolution has proven its capacity to stand up to challenges, its capacity to fight and its capacity to resist whatever it has to; that is what has turned us into an invincible people. These are our principles. Our Revolution is based on ideas and persuasion, and not on the use of force. I hope there is not anyone in the world crazy enough to say that 1.2 million people were forced to march along the sea front drive on July 26.

That has been our reaction, and we wanted our people to see the scenes and watch the tragedy. We have not hesitated to express our sentiments publicly, and right here I have a statement, which was drafted as soon as the facts were known and handed out to the international media around 3:00 p.m.

In the meantime, our television networks were broadcasting news of the events. This statement was scheduled to be read to the Cuban public tonight during the evening TV newscast.

I am going to move the time up a few minutes by reading to you here and now the Official Statement from the Government of Cuba on the events that took place in the United States:

"The Government of the Republic of Cuba has learned with grief and sadness of the violent surprise attacks carried out this morning against civilian and official facilities in the cities of New York and Washington, which have caused numerous deaths.

"Cuba's position against any terrorist action is well known." Our history proves that, and those who know the history of our revolutionary struggles know it well. "It is not possible to forget that for over four decades our country has been the target of such actions fostered from within the United States territory.

"Both for historical reasons and ethical principles, the Government of our country strongly repudiates and condemns the attacks against the aforementioned facilities and hereby expresses its most heartfelt sympathies to the American people for the painful, unjustifiable loss of human lives resulting from these attacks.

"In this bitter hour for all Americans, our people express their solidarity with the American people and their full willingness to cooperate, to the extent of their modest possibilities, with the health care institutions and any other medical or humanitarian organization in that country in the treatment, care and rehabilitation of the victims of this morning's events."

This message has not only been made public, but has also been officially delivered this afternoon, especially when we started to hear of the impressive numbers of possible casualties, and knew that hospitals were full of injured.

Although it is not known whether the casualties are 5000; 10,000; 15,000 or 20,000, it is known that the planes that crashed into the Twin Towers and into the Pentagon were carrying hundreds of passengers, and we have offered to provide whatever we can, if necessary.

That is a country with great scientific and medical development and resources, but at some point in time it could need blood of a specific type or plasma —any other product that we could donate, we would be most willing to give— or medical support or paramedics. We know many hospitals are short of specific technicians and professionals. In other words, we want to express our disposition and readiness to be helpful in relation to these tragic events.

There is a history to all of this, because as I said, we have been affected by terrorism for more than forty years. We have even published that on specific occasions we have informed the U.S. government of serious risks to the lives of Americans. Here is an example; it is a page and a quarter long.

After the terrorist attacks against our hotels by the terrorist mob in Florida that organized and paid for the terrorist attacks against Cuba, as well as the assassination plots organized against me when I have needed to travel abroad, a group headed by that monster Posada Carriles —we had already caught some of his accomplices, who were foreign mercenaries, when they entered our national territory— intended to repeat the sophisticated procedure used with the bombs planted in hotels or places frequently visited by foreign tourists, like La Bodeguita del Medio Restaurant, that could explode up to 99 hours after being set up. They could travel here, plant the bomb on the plane, party for three days, and go back to their country before the bomb exploded. There was the case of a Salvadoran mercenary who planted five bombs in hotels and other public places and attempted to make them blow up almost simultaneously, one after the other. You can see how far they had gone.

We made contact with the U.S. Government more than once through confidential channels, and here I have one of the direct messages that we sent to the President at that time. These were messages sent through confidential channels, not official ones, through fully trustworthy friends of ours who were also friends of his, and we precisely explained everything that we wanted them to convey. Part of this information has already been released to the public, but I will give you an example:

"An important issue.

"Number one: Plans for terrorist actions against Cuba continue to be hatched and paid by the Cuban American National Foundation using Central

American mercenaries. Two new attempts at setting up bombs in tourist resorts have been undertaken before, and after, the Pope's visit.

"In the first case, those responsible failed, they were able to escape and return to Central America by plane leaving behind the technical means and explosives which were then seized.

"In the second case, three mercenaries were arrested with explosives and other means. They are Guatemalans. They would have received 1500 USD for every bomb exploded." These were among the first caught, not the one who planted the most bombs.

"In both cases they were hired and supplied by agents of the ring organized by the Cuban American National Foundation. Now, they are plotting and taking steps to set up bombs in planes from Cuba or any other country airline carrying tourists to, or from, Cuba to Latin American countries.

"The method is similar: to hide a small device at a certain place inside the plane, a powerful explosive with a fuse controlled by a digital clock that can be programmed 99 hours in advance, then easily abandon the plane at foreseen destination; the explosion would take place either on the ground or while the plane is in flight to its next destination. Really devilish procedures: easy to handle mechanisms, components whose detection is practically impossible, a minimum training required for their use, almost absolute impunity. Extremely dangerous to airlines and to tourist facilities or of any other type. Tools suitable for a crime, very serious crimes.

"If they were revealed and their possibilities exposed," —we were opposed to revealing the technology used— "they might become an epidemic as the hijacking of planes once became. Other Cuban extremist groups living in the United States are beginning to move in that direction.

"The American investigation and intelligence agencies are in possession of enough reliable information on the main people responsible. If they really want to, they have the possibility of preventing in time this new modality of terrorism. It will be impossible to stop it if the United States doesn't discharge its fundamental duty of fighting it. The responsibility to fight it can't be left to Cuba alone since any other country of the world might also be a victim of such actions."

We passed this information on to them, and they paid so much attention that they even consulted with us on the advisability of sending airlines a text issued by the U.S. Government.

They sent us the text in which the airlines were informed of the following: "We have received unconfirmed information of a plot to place explosive devices aboard civilian aircraft operating between Cuba and Latin American countries. Those involved in the plot plan to leave behind a small explosive device aboard an aircraft..." Basically, they explained what we had informed them of.

"We cannot discount the possibility that the threat could include international air carrier operations from the United States.

"The U.S. Government continues to seek further information to clarify, and substantiate or refute, this threat."

We expressed our opposition to issuing that kind of warning because one of the objectives of those individuals was to create panic. We also explained that there were other procedures that we used. We set up the appropriate watch systems wherever there was any risk of bombs, we searched and knew who could plant them and who were involved. We kept watching, which is what has to be done, if you do not want to grow panic or make a scandal or grant the perpetrators the possibility to attain their objective, which was to impinge on the economy of the country and sow terror.

Anyway, they published the information. That was fine with us since we had already strengthened our mechanisms to capture those individuals. They have not even been able to plant a small bomb ever since, and the watch system remains in place where necessary. When they plotted the assassination attempt in Panama, we knew more than they were planning, and more than they knew. That is for sure.

There is the Miami Mafia making efforts to release the terrorists caught "*in fraganti*" and arrested in Panama. They have already planned how to do it and the country through which they would evacuate them and how. They would pretend to be sick and be moved. They freely receive visitors from Miami. We even know that they contributed to an infiltration through Santa Clara a few months ago.

Thanks to many friends that we have everywhere and to men like those (he points to the pictures of the Cuban patriots incarcerated in Miami for seeking information on terrorist plan against Cuba), the country has been able to defend itself from that terrorism.

I say this here because the truth is that there are more papers and notes, and we have sometimes sent verbal messages, and sometimes we have left written evidence, and one of the arguments that we have used is irrefutable: The United States is the country with the largest number of extremist organized groups, 400 of which are armed.

The hijacking of planes —a method used against Cuba— became a universal plague, and it was Cuba that solved this problem when, after repeated warnings, we sent two hijackers back to the United States. It is painful because they were Cubans but we had issued public warnings, so they came and we returned them. We complied with our public pledge, yet they never again provided us with any information about them to give to their relatives. They have their own ways of doing this. No one knows what they will do. I know they were sentenced to 40 years imprisonment, and that put an end to those hijackings.

But, listen, they have 800 groups of extremists. Sometimes they have locked themselves in a place for a certain reason and have burned themselves to death. They have groups, which due to political or sometimes religious reasons are prone to the use of force or to prepare poisons and products to act against the U.S. authorities. I am not talking about the Mafia people. I am talking about the hundreds of extremist organized groups acting within the United States. They blew up that building in Oklahoma not so long ago.

The United States is the country that is most vulnerable to terrorism; it is the country with more planes, more dependable on technical resources, electric grids, pipelines, etceteras. Many members of these groups are fascists and they do not mind killing. Mentally speaking, they must be closer to madness than to a balanced intelligence. We have said to the U.S. authorities that it is necessary to avoid the dissemination of these methods, we use that argument because they are easy to use and a danger for that country.

At this very moment, I mean, as I arrived here, there was no element of judgment to say who could have exploded those bombs, because it could have been an action planned and carried out by any of these groups, which have already done it before, like in the case of Oklahoma, or it could have been done by groups from abroad. However, it is evident —based on the details received— that it was effectively organized, in other words, with sufficient organization and synchronization, by people who have the knowledge, the training and by pilots who were able to drive these huge Boeings, by people who coordinated the exact times at which they would act. They undoubtedly hijacked the planes, diverting them from their planned route; and had the pilots who could drive the planes directly against one tower or other targets and some minutes later against the other, and nearly at the same time, a third plane was crashed against the Pentagon.

In other words, they are very well trained and organized people and not necessarily operating in large groups. It is impossible to imagine the damage that can be caused by a small group of 20; 25 or 30 people, who are extremists devoted to certain ideas, and it is in the United States where they can cause most damage. You can perceive how they studied the time at which more people would be in the offices, around 9:00 am, the damage they could make, and the thousands of casualties they could provoke.

Actually, given the special characteristics of this event, it is now necessary to look for clues. That is the reason why I believe the most important duty of American leaders is to fight terrorism, and these tragedies are partly the result of the use of terrorist methods against other countries, like in the case of Cuba and other countries for a number of years. The idea of terrorism has been disseminated, and there is no power in the world today, regardless its size, that can avoid events of this nature because bigots, people who are totally indifferent to death, carry them out. Thus, the struggle against such methods is difficult.

A lesson can be drawn from that: none of the problems affecting today's world can be solved with the use of force, there is no global, technological or military power that can guarantee total immunity against such acts, because they can be organized by small groups, difficult to detect, and what is more complicated, carried out by suicidal people. Therefore, the general effort of the international community must be to put an end to a number of conflicts affecting the world, at least in this area. It is indispensable to put an end to world terrorism and build a worldwide awareness against terrorism. I speak on behalf of a country, which has lived through more than 40 years of Revolution, and has gained much experience, a unified country with a high cultural level. It is not a country of bigots. Here, it is not fanaticism that has been cultivated but ideas, convictions and principles.

We could be in a better position to defend ourselves, and we have demonstrated it. How many lives we have saved while so much money and resources have been used to bring terrorism to our homeland! We have 40 years of experience, so we are ten times better prepared than the United States to prevent such actions.

It is very important to know what will be the reaction of the U.S. Government. Possibly the days to come will be dangerous for the world, and I do not mean Cuba. Cuba is the most peaceful country in the world for several reasons: our policy, our kind of struggle, our doctrine, and also, comrades, for the absolute absence of fear.

Nothing troubles us. Nothing intimidates us. It would be very difficult to put together a package against Cuba, not even its inventor and the patent holder would believe it, this is very difficult and today Cuba means something to the world. Cuba has a very high moral position, and a very sound political position in the world. It does not even cross my mind, although there is one of those Mafia fools trying to scheme something who I think even mentioned Venezuela and Cuba; one of the so many Mafiosi, a despicable big mouth. But, no one will pay the slightest attention, even though there will be tension and risks, depending on how the U.S. Government proceeds.

The days to come will be tense both inside and outside the United States. A number of people will start to express their views.

Whenever there is a tragedy like this one, no matter how difficult to avoid it may be, I see no other way but to keep calm. And if at some point I am allowed to make a suggestion to an adversary who has been tough with us for many years, but knows we can be tough too, knows we resist, and knows we are not stupid and there is a little respect for our people, if under specific circumstances it were correct to suggest something to the adversary, for the well being of the American people and based on the arguments I have given you, we would advise the leaders of the powerful empire to keep their equanimity, to act calmly, not to be carried away by a fit of rage or hatred and not to start hunting people down dropping bombs just anywhere.

I reiterate that none of the world problems —not even terrorism— can be solved with the use of force, and every act of force, every imprudent action that entails the use of force anywhere would seriously aggravate the world problems.

The way is neither the use of force nor the war.

I say this here with the full authority of someone who has always been honest, with the sound conviction and the experience of someone who has been through the years of struggle that we have lived in Cuba. It is only guided by reason and applying an intelligent policy based on the strength of consensus and the support of the international public opinion that such a predicament could definitely be solved. I think this unexpected episode must be used to undertake an international struggle against terrorism. However, this international struggle against terrorism cannot succeed by killing a terrorist here and another one there, that is, by using similar methods to theirs, sacrificing innocent lives. It is resolved, *inter alia*, by putting an end to State terrorism and other repulsive crimes, by putting an end to genocide and by honestly pursuing a policy of peace and respect for unavoidable moral and legal standards. The world cannot be saved unless a path of international peace and cooperation is pursued.

Nobody should think that we are trying to buy a ton of any thing in the U.S. market. We have proven that we can survive, live and make progress, and everything seen here today is an expression of an unprecedented progress in history. Progress is not achieved only through the manufacturing of automobiles; developing people's minds, providing knowledge and culture, and looking after human beings accordingly makes progress. That is the secret of the tremendous strength of our Revolution.

The world cannot be saved any other way, and I mean from violent situations. May peace be accomplished everywhere to protect all the peoples from that plague of terrorism, which is one of the plagues, because there is another horrible plague today, which is called AIDS, for instance. There is another plague, which kills tens of millions of children, teenagers and people in the world, that is, starvation, diseases and lack of medical care and medications.

In the political area, there are absolutist ideas, a single way of thinking that they try to impose on the world thus promoting rebellious attitudes and irritation everywhere.

This world cannot be saved —and this has nothing to do with terrorism— if this unfair economic and social order continues to be developed and applied leading the world to a catastrophe, to a blind alley for the 6.2 billion people who live today on this planet which is increasingly destroyed and led to poverty, unemployment, hunger and despair. The masses in different historical places like Seattle, Quebec, Washington and Genoa have proven that.

We expressed our opposition to publishing that kind of warning, because one of the goals of those individuals was to create panic. We also explained that there were other procedures that could be followed, like the ones that we use: we set up the appropriate watch systems wherever there was any risk of bombs, we searched and knew who could plant them and who was involved in these plans. We kept watching, which is what has to be done, if you do not want to spread panic or create a scandal or grant the perpetrators the possibility to achieve their goal, which was to damage the country's economy and sow terror.

In any case, they published the information. That is fine with us, we had already strengthened our mechanisms to capture those individuals, they have not even been able to plant a small bomb ever since, and the watch system is still in place where necessary. When they plotted the assassination attempt in Panama, we knew more than they themselves did about what they were planning. That is for sure.

Now the Miami mob is working on freeing the terrorists caught in *flagrante delicto* and arrested in Panama. They have already planned how to do it, which country they will evacuate them through and how. They will feign an illness and then make their move. They are freely receiving visitors from Miami, and even participated in the sending of armed infiltrators to Cuba, through Santa Clara, some months ago.

Thanks to the many friends that we have everywhere and to men like those (he points to the pictures of the Cuban patriots imprisoned in Miami for gathering information on terrorist plans against Cuba), the country has been able to defend itself against terrorism.

I am pointing this out here because there is a reality, there are more papers and notes, and we have sometimes sent verbal messages, and sometimes we have left written evidence, and one of the arguments that we have used is irrefutable: the United States is the country with the largest number of organized extremist groups, and 400 of them are armed.

The hijacking of airplanes —a method invented for use against Cuba— became a universal plague, and it was Cuba that ultimately solved this problem when, after repeated warnings, we sent two hijackers back to the United States. It was painful, because they were Cubans, but we had issued public warnings, they came here and we returned them. We complied with our public pledge and yet they never again provided us with any information about them to pass on to their relatives. They have their own way of acting. I know they were sentenced to 40 years imprisonment, and that put an end to the hijacking of airplanes.

But listen, they have 800 extremist groups over there. At times they have locked themselves up some place for some reason and they have burn themselves to death. There are groups formed for many reasons, often political, sometimes religious, that are prone to violence and the use of force, or the poisoning of products as a means to take action against the US authorities. I am not talking about the mob people. I am talking about hundreds of organized extremist groups acting within the United States. They blew up that building in Oklahoma not so long ago.

The United States is the country most vulnerable to terrorism. It is the country with the most planes, with the greatest dependence on technical resources, electrical power grids, gas pipelines, and so on. Many of the people in these groups are fascists who do not mind killing. Mentally speaking, they must be closer to insanity than to a balanced intelligence. We have told the U.S. authorities that these methods should not be publicized, because they are easy to use and a danger for them.

As I arrived here, there was no evidence as to who could have planted those bombs, because it may have been an action planned and carried out by any of these groups, which have already done such things, like in the case of Oklahoma, or it may have been done by groups from abroad. However, it is evident, based on the details received, that it was very effectively organized, in other words, with a high degree of organization and synchronization, by people who have the knowledge and the training, and by pilots who were able to handle these large Boeings, by people who coordinated the exact time at which they were going to act. They undoubtedly hijacked the planes, diverting them from their scheduled routes, and had pilots who could steer the planes directly into a tower or other target, and then the other tower a few minutes later, and at nearly the same time, another against the Pentagon.

In other words, they are people who are very well trained and organized, and they do not necessarily need to be from large groups. It is unimaginable the damage that can be caused by a small group of 20; 25 or 30 people, who are extremist fanatics fully devoted to certain ideas, and the place where they can do the most damage is the United

States. You can see how they studied the time at which more people would be in the offices, around 9:00 a.m., the damage they could do, and the thousands of casualties they could cause.

In fact, they now have to look for clues, any clues, because this event has special characteristics. That is the reason why I believe the most important duty of U.S. leaders is to fight terrorism, and these tragedies are partly the result of the use of terrorist methods against other countries, as in the case of Cuba for so many years. The idea of terrorism has been broadly disseminated, and there is no power in the world today, regardless of its size, that can avoid events of this nature, because the bigots who carry them out are totally indifferent to death. Thus, the struggle against such methods is difficult.

A lesson can be drawn from this: none of the problems affecting today's world can be solved with the use of force; there is no global, technological or military power that can guarantee immunity against such acts, because they can be organized by small groups, difficult to detect, and what is more complicated, used by suicidal people. Therefore, the general effort of the international community must be to put an end to a number of conflicts affecting the world, at least in this area; there should be an end to world terrorism while a worldwide awareness is built. I speak on behalf of a country that has lived through more than 40 years of Revolution and has gained much experience, a unified country with a high cultural level. This is not a country of bigots. It has not been bigotry but rather ideas, convictions and principles that have been cultivated here.

We are in a better position to defend ourselves, and we have demonstrated it. Just look at the number of lives we have saved while so much money and resources have been used to sow terrorism in our homeland! We have 40 years of experience, so we are ten times better prepared than the United States to prevent such episodes.

It is very important to know what the reaction of the U.S. Government might be. Possibly the world will be living dangerous days, and I am not talking about Cuba. Cuba is the most peaceful country in the world, for several reasons: our policies, our forms of struggle, our doctrine, our ethics, and also, comrades, and due to an absolute absence of fear.

Nothing troubles us. Nothing intimidates us. It would be very difficult to concoct a slanderous accusation against Cuba; not even its inventor and the patent holder would believe it. It would be very difficult. And Cuba means something in the world today. It has a very high moral position, and a very sound political position in the world. I cannot even conceive of such a thing, although one of those mob fools is already attempting to scheme, and I think he even mentioned Venezuela and Cuba; one of the many members of that mob, one of those contemptible charlatans. No one will pay the slightest attention to him, but there will be tension and danger, depending on the U.S. Government's reaction.

The days to come will be tense both inside and outside the United States. A number of people will start putting forward opinions.

Whenever there is a tragedy like this, no matter how difficult to avoid it may be, I see no other way but to remain calmed. And if at some point I were allowed to make a suggestion to the adversary who has been so tough on us for many years, but who knows we are tough, knows we resist, and knows we are not stupid, and there is just a little respect for our people, but if under certain circumstances it were correct to suggest something to the adversary, for the well-being of the American people and based on the arguments I have given you, we would advise the leaders of that powerful empire to remain calm, to act with a cool head, to avoid getting carried away by a fit of rage or hatred, and not to start trying to hunt people down by throwing bombs just anywhere.

I reiterate that none of the world's problems, not even terrorism, can be solved with the use of force, and every act of force, every imprudent action that entails the use of force anywhere, is going to seriously aggravate the world problems.

The way is neither the use of force nor the war. I say this with the full authority of someone who has always talked honestly, of someone with sound convictions and the experience of surviving the years of struggle that Cuba has lived through. Only reason, and the intelligent policy of seeking strength through consensus and international public opinion, can definitely eradicate this problem. I think this unexpected episode should be used to undertake an international effort against terrorism. However, this international struggle against terrorism cannot be won by eliminating a terrorist here and another one there, by killing people here and there, using similar methods to theirs and sacrificing innocent lives. It can only be won, among other ways, by putting an end to State terrorism and other repulsive forms of killing, by putting an end to genocide, and by seriously pursuing a policy of peace and respect for moral and legal standards. The world cannot be saved unless a path of international peace and cooperation is pursued.

Nobody should think that we are trying to buy a ton of anything on the U.S. market. We have proven that we can survive, live and make progress, and everything seen here today is an expression of unprecedented progress in all of human history. Progress is not achieved only through the manufacturing of automobiles; developing people's minds, providing knowledge, promoting culture, and looking after human beings the way they should be looked after makes progress. That is the secret of the tremendous strength of our Revolution.

The world cannot be saved in any other way, and by that I mean the situations of violence. Let us seek peace everywhere and protect all the people from that plague of terrorism, which is only one of the plagues, because there is another horrible plague today, which is called AIDS, for instance. There is another plague, which kills tens of millions of children, teenagers and adults in the world, that is, hunger, disease and a lack of health care and medicines.

In the political arena, there are absolutist ideas, and attempts to impose a single way of thinking on the world; this fosters rebellious attitudes and irritation everywhere.

This world cannot be saved —and this does not have anything to do with terrorism— if this unfair economic and social order continues to be developed and applied; an order that is leading the world to disaster, along a path from which there is no escape for the 6.2 billion people living today and the future inhabitants of this planet, suffering ever greater destruction and plunged further into poverty, unemployment, hunger and despair. This has been proven by the masses in places that have already gone down in history, like Seattle, Quebec, Washington and Genoa.

The world's most powerful economic and political leaders now find it almost impossible to meet; everywhere we can see that people are less and less afraid, and are rising up. I was recently in Durban and there I saw thousands and thousands of people members of non-governmental organizations; discontent is spreading like wildfire around the globe.

Now that I have already mentioned one of the plagues, it is only fair to talk of the others, and the most influential national leaders are obliged to seek for a solution to a situation that worsens by the minute. A serious economic crisis is affecting the whole planet; it gravely affects the United States, Europe, Japan, and the industrialized nations of Southeast Asia, with virtually the sole exception of China. Alongside its economic reforms, China has maintained distribution methods that prevent hunger in a country with the largest number of inhabitants on earth but only 5% of the world's agricultural land, proving that the world can still be saved.

The crisis is profound. Every day in the news we read of what is happening on the stock exchanges, of fluctuations in currency values, of increases in unemployment, of reductions in growth, and almost no one can escape, with the above-mentioned exceptions and perhaps another one under very special circumstances.

It is serious crisis and it could be worse than that of 1929, because speculation has been abused more than in 1929. Almost infinite but artificial wealth has been created, stock prices have been inflated, so much so that those who invested $1000 in one or various shares have watched their value rise to $800 000 in eight or nine years. But it is imaginary money, and the companies whose shares have undergone the most rapid growth have lost more than half of their value.

We watch the theorists and analysts inventing things, old and new remedies that have no impact on the crisis but bring more and more surprises. No one can predict the outcome, but I can assure you that the situation is very complex for the world economy, for neoliberalism, for neoliberal globalization.

The power of the large transnationals is ever greater; they are more independent and tend to act wantonly. Even governments are increasingly unable to fight and resist them.

You cannot imagine how the scenario has changed in just four months, between the last quarter of 2000 and this month. During this year there have been periods of favorable economic winds in Europe, but the wind has died, the wind no longer blows over Europe, all is calm and the tide is changing.

It is amazing to see the things that are happening in Japan, a country that was so capable of developing itself that for years everything that it did was called a miracle, and yet now its problems are worse every day.

Nobody can say with any precision what will happen and how it will happen, because although events arise in almost mathematical fashion, economics is not an exact science. Trends, nevertheless, are clear and irrefutable. The prices for basic commodities are at rock bottom and ever more complicated situations continue to emerge. They know this, as do the Europeans and their economic strategists.

In recent weeks the United States has reduced its interest rate six times. This is one mechanism they use to check whether there is more money in the system and if people will buy more, in order for industries to produce more, even if resources are wasted.

It is an economy that needs people to throw more and more money away in order to survive. It is not an economy that serves humankind; it only serves itself and the owners of the giant companies, not the people.

We have to contend with all these problems on a daily basis. We need to know if the price of oil has gone up, or down, if the sugar price has fallen more. We need detailed daily information on what is happening in the world, and so we observe and review the situation every day.

[...]

STATEMENT FROM THE GOVERNMENT OF THE REPUBLIC OF CUBA

The Government of the Republic of Cuba has received with pain and sadness the news of the violent and surprise attacks this morning on civilian and official installations in the cities of New York and Washington, and the resultant numerous casualties.

Cuba´s position against any act of terrorism is well known. It is impossible to forget that our people have been the victims of such actions, promoted from U.S. territory itself, for more than 40 years.

For both historical reasons and etnical principles, the government of our country totally rejects and condemns the attacks mounted on the above-mentioned installations and offers its sincerest condolences to the U.S. people for the painful and unjustified human losses those attacks provoked.

At this bitter time, our people express their solidarity with the U.S. people and their total disposition to cooperate, as far as their modest possibilities allow, with that country´s public health or any other institution of a medical or humanitarian nature, in terms of attention, care and rehabilitation of the victims of this morning´s incidents.

City of Havana, September 11, 2001

EVERYTHING IS NOT LOST, YET

Under the effect of the shock caused to the world by the appalling and brutal terrorist action that targeted the American people on September 11, underlined by painful reports and images of grief and sorrow, certain minds driven by feelings of hatred and arrogance have taken to the sinister task of reviving old methods and doctrines which lie at the very source of terrorism and the extremely grave tensions affecting the world today.

At a time when the only advisable thing to do is to calmly and courageously seek for a definitive solution to terrorism and other tragedies, by universal consensus, a rude language full of rage and a spirit of vengeance, that had not been heard since the days prior to World War II, is being used by influential political leaders in the United States.

Any honest person would have the right to ask if it is really justice what they want or rather to use the hurting and outrageous tragedy to impose methods, prerogatives and privileges leading to the establishment of an unrestricted tyranny over every people on Earth by the most powerful state in the world.

Some senior officials have openly claimed that all restrictions should be lifted on the right of American institutions and officials to murder any person, even if that requires the use of the most despicable criminals. Such a prerogative had been used in the past by U.S. leaders to eliminate patriots like Patricio Lumumba in 1961, and to arrange coup d'état and carnage which have taken the lives of hundreds of thousands and millions who have been tortured, vanished or removed by diverse means.

Cuba has denounced hundreds of plans of assassinate its leaders and has tirelessly demanded punishment for those responsible and for the authors of countless acts of terrorism which have claimed a high number of human lives from our people. The very U.S. Senate investigated and exposed several actions carried out against Cuba using various means that did not leave out any form of murder no matter how uncouth and revolting. A peculiar kind of science was developed to that end.

The world has not given its unanimous support or expressed its most sincere condolences to the noble American people to let such sentiments be used to elaborate doctrines that would spread chaos and bloody events throughout the planet. The fact that a State proclaims an alleged right to kill wantonly anywhere in the world in contempt of legal procedures, courts of law or even the presentation of evidence is as serious as terrorism itself, and one its most despicable manifestations. Such policy would constitute a barbarian and uncivilized action that would tear to pieces every rule and legal bases on which peace and coexistence between nations might be built.

Amidst the panic and confusion created by this whole situation and despite the extreme gravity of introducing such procedures in international affairs, the political leaders of various states have failed to speak out —with few exceptions— against the emergence of a fascist and terrorist trend implicit in such statements.

One of the first consequences of this has been the acts of xenophobia and terror perpetrated against people of a different nationality or religion. Although terrorism is absolutely repugnant and immoral, the American people would never favor the brutal method of murdering other people in cool blood, breaking the law, punishing without evidence or denying fundamental principles of equity and justice with the pretext of fighting it. Such methods would take the planet back to law of the jungle, tarnish the United States' reputation and destroy its prestige while further inciting the hatred that is today at the root of so much grief and sadness. The American people want justice, not revenge!

Cuba said from the very first moment that in today's world no problem can be solved with the use of force and that, in order to fight terrorism, it was necessary to build an awareness and a universal union capable of definitely eradicating this and other scourges and tragedies that put in jeopardy the very survival of the specie.

Although the war drums beat unexpectedly loud and they seem to irrevocably lead towards a bloody end, everything is not lost, yet.

In Afghanistan the ulemas —religious leaders of a traditionally combative and brave people— are meeting to adopt fundamental decisions. They have already said that they will not oppose the application of justice and the relevant procedures if those accused, living in their country, are really guilty. They have simply asked for evidence, and for guarantees of impartiality and equity in the process, something that the United Nations could perfectly ensure, with full support from the international community.

If such evidence exists, as the leaders of the U.S. government have categorically affirmed, and the religious leaders are not asked to override the deepest convictions of their faith, which they are known to defend with their own lives, then an alternative to war could be worked out. They would not sacrify their people uselessly if their ethically unquestionable request was taken into account. In fact, a bloodshed could be avoided and this could become the first great step towards a world without terrorism or unpunished crimes: a true world association for peace and justice could emerge and the American people would earn enormous prestige and respect.

Cuba would resolutely support such a solution. But, there is not a minute to spare; there is little time left. To fail to make such a basic, simple and viable effort would make it an unjust war.

By the Government of the Republic of Cuba

Havana, September 19, 2001

SPEECH AT THE OPEN FORUM OF THE REVOLUTION

San Antonio de Los Baños, Havana, september 22, 2001

Fellow countrymen:

No one can deny that terrorism is today a dangerous and ethically indefensible phenomenon, which should be eradicated regardless of its deep origins, the economic and political factors that brought it to live and those responsible for it.

The unanimous irritation caused by the human and psychological damage brought on the American people by the unexpected and shocking death of thousands of innocent people whose images have shaken the world is perfectly understandable. But who have profited? The extreme right, the most backward and right-wing forces, those in favor of crushing the growing world rebellion and sweeping away everything progressive that is still left on the planet. It was an enormous error, a huge injustice and a great crime whomever they are who organized or are responsible for such action.

However, the tragedy should not be used to recklessly start a war that could actually unleash an endless carnage of innocent people and all of this on behalf of justice and under the peculiar and bizarre name of "Infinite Justice".

In the last few days we have seen the hasty establishment of the basis, the concept, the true purposes, the spirit and the conditions for such a war. No one would be able to affirm that it was not something thought out well in advance, something that was just waiting for its chance to materialize. Those who after the so-called end of the cold war continued a military build-up and the development of the most sophisticated means to kill and exterminate human beings were aware that the large military investments would give them the privilege to impose an absolute and complete dominance over the other peoples of the world. The ideologists of the imperialist system knew very well what they were doing and why they were doing it.

After the shock and sincere sorrow felt by every people on Earth for the atrocious and insane terrorist attack that targeted the American people, the most extremist ideologists and the most belligerent hawks, already set in privileged power positions, have taken command of the most powerful country in the world whose military and technological capabilities would seem infinite. Actually, its capacity to destroy and kill is enormous while its inclination towards equanimity, serenity, thoughtfulness and restrain is minimal.

The combination of elements —including complicity and the common enjoyment of privileges— the prevailing opportunism, confusion and panic make it almost impossible to avoid a bloody and unpredictable outcome.

The first victims of whatever military actions are undertaken will be the billions of people living in the poor and underdeveloped world with their unbelievable economic and social problems, their unpayable debts and the ruinous prices of their basic commodities; their growing natural and ecological catastrophes, their hunger and misery, the massive undernourishment of their children, teenagers and adults; their terrible AIDS epidemic, their malaria, their tuberculosis and their infectious diseases that threaten whole nations with extermination.

The grave economic world crisis was already a real and irrefutable fact affecting absolutely every one of the big economic power centers. Such crisis will inevitably grow deeper under the new circumstances and when it becomes unbearable for the overwhelming majority of the peoples, it will bring chaos, rebellion and the impossibility to govern.

But the price will also be unpayable for the rich countries. For years to come it would be impossible to speak strong enough about the environment and the ecology, or about ideas and research done and tested, or about projects for the protection of Nature because that space and possibility would be taken by military actions, war and crimes as infinite as "Infinite Justice", that is, the name given to the war operation to be unleashed.

Can there be any hope left after having listened, hardly 36 hours ago, to the speech made the President before de U.S. Congress?

I will avoid the use of adjectives, qualifiers or offensive words towards the author of that speech. They would be absolutely unnecessary and untimely when the tensions and seriousness of the moment advise thoughtfulness and equanimity. I will limit myself to underline some short phrases that say it all:

"We will use every necessary weapon of war."

"Americans should not expect one battle, but a lengthy campaign unlike any other we have ever seen."

"Every nation in every region now has a decision to make. Either you are with us or you are with the terrorists."

"I've called the armed forces to alert and there is a reason. The hour is coming when America will act and you will make us proud."

"This is the world's fight, this is civilization's fight."

"I ask for your patience [...] in what will be a long struggle."

"The great achievement of our time and the great hope of every time, now depend on us."

"The course of this conflict is not known, yet its outcome is certain. [...] And we know that God is not neutral."

I ask our fellow countrymen to meditate deeply and calmly on the ideas contained in several of the above-mentioned phrases:

- Either you are with us or you are with the terrorists.
- No nation of the world has been left out of the dilemma, not even the big and powerful states; none has escaped the threat of war or attacks.
- We will use any weapon.
- No procedure has been excluded, regardless of its ethics, or any threat whatever fatal, either nuclear, chemical, biological or any other.
- It will not be short combat but a lengthy war, lasting many years, unparalleled in history.
- It is the world's fight; it is civilization's fight.
- The achievements of our times and the hope of every time, now depend on us.

Finally, an unheard of confession in a political speech on the eve of a war, and no less than in times of apocalyptic risks: The course of this conflict is not known; yet its outcome is certain. And we know that God is not neutral.

This is an amazing assertion. When I think about the real or imagined parties involved that bizarre holy war that is about to begin, I find it difficult to make a distinction about where fanaticism is stronger.

On Thursday, before the United States

Congress, the idea was designed of a world military dictatorship under the exclusive rule of force, irrespective of any international laws or institutions. The United Nations Organization, simply ignored in the present crisis, would fail to have any authority or prerogative whatsoever. There would be only one boss, only one judge, and only one law.

We have all been ordered to ally either with the United States government or with terrorism.

Cuba, the country that has suffered the most and the longest from terrorist actions, the one whose people are not afraid of anything because there is no threat or power in the world that can intimidate it, with a high morale Cuba claims that it is opposed to terrorism and opposed to war. Although the possibilities are now remote, Cuba reaffirms the need to avert a war of unpredictable consequences whose very authors have admitted not to have the least idea of how the events will unfold. Likewise, Cuba reiterates its willingness to cooperate with every country in the total eradication of terrorism.

An objective and calm friend should advise the United States government against throwing the young American soldiers into an uncertain war in remote, isolated and inaccessible places, like a fight against ghosts, not knowing where they are or even if they exist or not, or whether the people they kill are or not responsible for the death of their innocent fellow countrymen killed in the United States.

Cuba will never declare itself an enemy of the American people that is today subjected to an unprecedented campaign to sow hatred and a vengeful spirit, so much so that even the music that sings to peace has been banned. On the contrary, Cuba will make that music its own, and even our children will sing their songs to peace while the announced bloody war lasts.

Whatever happens, the territory of Cuba will never be used for terrorist actions against the American people and we will do everything within our reach to prevent such actions against that people. Today we are expressing our solidarity while urging to peace and calmness. One day they will admit we were right.

Our independence, our principles and our social achievements we will defend with honor to the last drop of blood, if we are attacked!

It will not be easy to fabricate pretexts to do it. They are already talking about a war using all the necessary weapons but it will be good recalling that not even that would be a new experience. Almost four decades ago, hundreds of strategic and tactical nuclear weapons were aimed at Cuba and nobody remembers anyone of our countrymen sleepless over that.

We are the same sons and daughters of that heroic people, with a patriotic and revolutionary conscience that is higher than ever. It is time for serenity and courage.

The world will grow aware of this and will raise

its voice in the face of the terrible threatening drama that it is about to suffer.

As for Cubans, this is the right time to proclaim more proud and resolute than ever:

Socialism or death!
Patria o muerte!
Venceremos!

SPEECH AT THE OPEN FORUM OF THE REVOLUTION

Ciego de Ávila, september 29, 2001

Fellow countrymen:

A peaceful solution would still be possible.
The present situation is so tense that nobody could write a speech hours before delivery and be certain that it is not outdated. I am also running the risk of sounding too optimistic even when I am not. However, it is my duty to say what I think.

The unanimous shock suffered by all peoples of the world on September 11, due to the insane terrorist attacks against the American people, which could be seen live on television, has created exceptional conditions for the eradication of terrorism without the need to unleash a useless and perhaps endless war.

Terrorist actions in the United States, as anywhere else in the world, inflict terrible damage on the peoples fighting for a cause that objectively they consider to be fair.

Terror has always been an instrument of the worst enemies of Mankind bent on suppressing and crushing the peoples' struggle for freedom. It can never be the instrument of a truly noble and just cause.

All throughout history, almost every action intended to attain national independence, including that of the American people, was carried out with the use of weapons and nobody ever questioned, or would question, that right. But, the deliberate use of weapons to kill innocent people must be definitely condemned and eradicated for it is as unworthy and inhuman as it is repulsive, the same as the historic terrorism perpetrated by the oppressing states.

In the present crisis, real possibilities still exist to eradicate terrorism without a war but the main obstacle is that the most notable political and military leaders in the United States refuse to listen to any word said against the use of weapons and in favor of a truly effective solution to the worrisome problem, heedless of the fact that it would be very honorable for the American people to accomplish that objective while avoiding blood shedding. The decision-makers are only betting on war actions. They have associated honor with war. Some speak of the use of nuclear weapons as if it were as simple as having a cup of tea. Others affirm that paratroopers will be employed in irregular warfare tactics. Someone has even speculated on the advisability of using lies as a weapon although others have shown more rationality and common sense but still along the war line. Objectivity and rationality are not abundant. Many people have been made to believe that only belligerent formulas are viable regardless the loss of American lives.

It is hard to know whether the final tactic and strategy of struggle have already been decided upon to use against a country whose communications and technological infrastructure as well as material conditions seem to have hardly left the Stone Age behind. Will irregular warfare tactics with squadrons of aircraft carriers, armored warships, cruisers and submarines be used in a landlocked country? Why send also scores of B-1 and B-52 bombers, hundreds of modern fighter planes, thousands of missiles and other strategic weapons? What are they going to shoot against?

Meanwhile, confusion and panic prevail in the rest of the world, while opportunistic positions motivated by convenience and national interests are not lacking. Some have torn their honor to pieces. And, following the initial atmosphere of uncertainty there is a bizarre and widespread ostrich reflex despite the fact that there are not even enough holes to hide heads.

Many seem not to have realized yet that, on September 20, before the United States Senate, the end of independence was decreed for every other state —without exceptions— as well as the end of the United Nations' role.

Nevertheless, no one should be misled into thinking that the peoples of the world, and a number of honest political leaders, will not react as soon as the war actions become a reality and their horrific images start to be seen. These will then take the place of the sad and shocking images of the events in New York at a time when forgetting them would bring irreparable damage on the spirit of solidarity with the American people that is today a primary element towards the eradication of terrorism, without the need to resort to a war of unpredictable consequences and avoiding the death of an incalculable number of innocents.

The first victims can already be seen. They are the millions trying to escape the war and the dying children with ghastly appearance whose images will move the world to pity without anyone being able to prevent their dissemination.

It is a great mistake on the part of the United States and its NATO allies to believe that the strong nationalism and religious sentiments of Muslims can be neutralized with either money or a promise of assistance, or that their countries can be permanently intimidated by force. There are already statements from religious leaders of major nations, that have no affinity whatsoever with the Taliban, who are voicing their resolute opposition to a military attack. Meanwhile, contradictions are beginning to arise among the United States' allies, both in Center and South East Asia.

On the other hand, xenophobia, hatred and scorn for every Muslim country are starting to emerge. An important European head of government has just said in Berlin that Western civilization is superior to Islamic and that the West will keep on conquering peoples, even if that means confrontation with the Islamic civilization, which has remained stuck where it was 1400 years ago.

In an economic situation such as the world is experiencing today, when extremely serious problems affecting Mankind remain unresolved, including its own survival which is threatened by other evils unrelated to the destructive power of modern weaponry, one wonders: Why this obstinate course of starting a complicated and open-ended war? Why are the American leaders showing such arrogance when their enormous power gives them the privilege of showing some moderation?

It would suffice to return to the United Nations Organization the prerogatives that it has been deprived of and let the General Assembly, its most universal and representative body, be the center of that fight for peace —regardless of its limitations due to the arbitrary veto right of the Security Council standing members, most of them also a part of NATO— and for the eradication of terrorism with total and unanimous support from the world opinion.

Under no circumstances should those responsible for the brutal attacks against the American people be allowed to go unpunished, if they can be identified. An honorable condition for every country would be that they are tried by an unbiased court of law that would ensure the reliability of the evidence and that justice be done.

Cuba was the first country to speak of the need for an international struggle against terrorism just a few hours after the tragedy brought on the American people on September 11. We also said that: "None of the present problems of the world can be solved by force. [...] The international community should build a world conscience against terrorism. [...] Only the intelligent policy of seeking strength through consensus and the international public opinion can decidedly uproot this problem [...] this unimaginable event should serve to launch an international struggle against terrorism. [...] The world cannot be saved unless a path of international peace and cooperation is pursued."

We firmly stand by these views.

It is indispensable to return to the United Nations its role in the attainment of peace.

I harbor no doubts that the Third World countries —I dare say almost everyone of them without exception, despite their political and religious differences— would be willing to go alongside the rest of the world in this struggle against terrorism as an alternative to war.

I think that these ideas do not, in any way, tarnish the honor, the dignity and the predominant political or religious principles of any of the above-mentioned states.

I am not talking here on behalf of any of the poor and underdeveloped countries of the world. I am simply expressing my deepest conviction as I am aware of the tragedy of these peoples that have been exploited and humiliated for centuries where, even without a war, inherited poverty and underdevelopment, hunger and curable diseases are silently killing scores of millions of innocents every year.

For these people, saving peace with dignity, with independence and without a war is the cornerstone of the struggle that we should wage together for a truly just world of free peoples.

Cuba is not motivated by any economic interest or by opportunism, much less by any fear of threat, danger or risk. But this people that, as it is widely known, has most honorably endured over four decades of economic warfare, blockade and terrorism is entitled to explain, reiterate and insist on its viewpoints; and, it will not hesitate to do so until the very last minute.

We are, and we will continue to be, opposed to terrorism and opposed to war! No matter what happens, nothing will separate us from that line!

The dark clouds on the horizon of the world today, will not prevent the Cubans from continuing to work restlessly on our wonderful social and cultural programs as we are persuaded that it is a human endeavor unparalleled in history. And even if the promised wars were to turn them into mere dreams, we would still fall with honor defending such dreams.

>Long live the Revolution and Socialism!
>Patria o Muerte!
>Venceremos!

DECLARATION BY THE NATIONAL ASSEMBLY OF PEOPLE'S POWER OF THE REPUBLIC OF CUBA

Twenty-five years ago Cuba was victim to a premeditated and heinous crime that shocked the whole nation and remains in the collective memory of our people.

On October 6, 1976, a Cubana Airline aircraft was the target of a cowardly act of sabotage that blew it up in mid flight offshore Barbados. All the passengers and crewmembers on board were killed, including the young winners of the Central American and Caribbean Fencing Championship and a group of Guyanese students. The 73 victims are still awaiting justice. The main culprits have never been brought to trial or sanctioned, thus they have continued to carry on their criminal careers for more than four decades.

Those who conceived, planned and directed this act of genocide have a long history of terrorism that began in the 1960's under the auspices of the CIA. The role they played in the blowing-up of the Cubana aircraft and the cold-blooded murder of all those on board are well known by the U.S. government. On June 23, 1989, the Department of Justice of that country admitted that it possessed information on the case, which it had kept a secret. Despite his infamous history, including serious crimes committed on American soil, contrary to the ruling of the Attorney General's Office and in spite of the opposition of major U.S. media, one of these terrorists, Orlando Bosch, has lived in the United States for more than ten years, thanks to a decision by the then-President George Bush, and there he has continued to carry out his monstrous trade undisturbed. This man and his cronies, confident of the complete impunity they enjoy and backed up by the so-called Cuban-American National Foundation announced, in a Miami daily paper full page last August 22, that they would continue to use all means and methods available against Cuba without ruling out either terrorism or violence.

After his escape from the Venezuelan penitentiary where he was awaiting trial in the case of the Cubana aircraft, the other terrorist, Luis Posada Carriles, immediately went to work for the White House. There, under direct orders from Lieut. Col. Oliver North, he became involved in the U.S. clandestine activities in Central America where he went on to direct various bomb-attacks against tourist resorts in Cuba and finally planned an assassination attempt against president Fidel Castro and thousands of Panamanian students meeting with him, on the occasion of last year's Ibero-American Summit. He is currently incarcerated in Panama awaiting trial on minor crimes; however, once again he is confident that his friends will ensure his freedom and impunity.

When the whole world repudiates the brutal attacks of last September 11, the United Nations adopts condemnatory resolutions and governments declare their intention to punish all such actions and avoid them ever being repeated, the National Assembly, alongside the Cuban people, condemns the attacks and reaffirms its solidarity with the American people while demanding that the war against terrorism be genuine, responding to a real desire to eradicate these acts wherever and however they occur.

Thousands of Cubans have lost their lives or suffered irreparable damage as a result of acts of vandalism perpetrated against Cuba for more than 40 years by groups who operated, and continue to operate, from inside the U.S. territory with the complicity or tolerance of that country's authorities. Cuba, on the other hand, has never resorted to such despicable methods nor ever used force against the bandits that have committed unspeakable atrocities against our people from foreign territory. We have always pursued a principled policy. We have defended ourselves without ever violating either the ethics or the principles of international law. Additionally, we have tried to make the government in Washington fulfill its obligation to prevent these terrorist acts, by supplying them with information obtained through the generous sacrifice of heroic countrymen like those who now languish in unjust incarceration in Miami.

We have every reason, and the necessary moral strength, to demand that justice also be done in the case of the crime committed on October 6, 1976. We strongly demand that the international struggle against terrorism be sincere, consistent, free from double standards, free from racism, free from hegemonic arrogance and free from fraudulent manipulation. This is the only way to completely eradicate this scourge; the only way to pay a most deserved tribute to all victims everywhere.

Twenty-five years ago, we were brought closely together like one large family by the pain and sorrow we felt when the lives of our brothers and sisters were so ruthlessly cut short. We pledged then that they would forever stay in our hearts, that they would never be forgotten; and, here they have been with us, always present in the sacrifice, the heroism, the dignity and the creative resistance of their people.

We shall continue to denounce their assassins and demand that they be punished. We will persevere in our struggle definitely united to defend our homeland and ensure that a free, independent, just and fraternal Cuba offers a permanent tribute to them and to all our martyrs.

Socialism or Death!
Homeland or Death!
We shall overcome!

National Assembly of People's Power
Havana, October 4, 2001
"Year of the Victorious Revolution in the New Millenium"

SPEECH AT THE OPEN FORUM OF THE REVOLUTION

Revolution Square, City of Havana, october 6, 2001

Fellow countrymen:

History can be unpredictable and move along strange labyrinths. Twenty-five years ago, in this very same square, we bid a final farewell to a small number of caskets. They contained tiny fragments of human remains and personal belongings of some of the 57 Cubans, 11 Guyanese —most of them students on scholarships in Cuba— and five North Korean cultural officials who were the victims of a brutal and inconceivable act of terrorism. What was particularly moving was the death of almost the entire Cuban juvenile fencing team, both women and men, coming home with every single one of the gold medals awarded in this sport at a Central American and Caribbean tournament.

A million of our fellow countrymen —as many as today— with tears filling their eyes and running down their cheeks, gathered here to bid a more symbolic than actual farewell to our brothers and sisters whose bodies rested on the ocean floor.

Nobody, except for a group of friendly personalities and institutions, shared our pain and sorrow. There was no upheaval around the world, no acute political crises, no United Nations meetings, nor the imminent threat of war.

Perhaps, few people in the world understood the terrible significance of that event. How important could it be that a Cuban jetliner was blown up in mid-flight with 73 people aboard? It was almost a common occurrence. Thousands of Cubans had already died in *La Coubre*, the Escambray Mountains, the Bay of Pigs, and in hundreds of other terrorist acts, pirate attacks and similar actions, had they not? Who could pay any attention to the denunciations of this tiny country? All that was needed, apparently, was a simple denial from the powerful neighbor and their media, which inundate the world, and the matter was forgotten.

Who could have predicted that almost exactly 25 years later, a war with totally unpredictable consequences would be on the verge of breaking out as a result of an equally heinous terrorist attack, which claimed the lives of thousands of innocent people in the United States? Back then, in what now appears to be a tragic omen, innocent people from various countries died; this time, there were victims from 86 nations.

Then, as now, there was hardly anything left of the victims. In Barbados, not a single body could be recovered and in New York, only a few were and not all of them identifiable. In both cases, the families were left with an appalling emptiness and infinite grief; a deep indignation and an unbearable sorrow was brought on the peoples of both nations. It had not been an accident, a mechanical failure or a human error; these were both deliberate acts, planned and executed in cold blood.

There were, however, a few differences between the monstrous crime in Barbados and the abhorrent, unimaginable terrorist attack against the American people. In the United States, the act was the work of fanatics willing to die alongside their victims, while in Barbados it was the work of mercenaries who did not run the slightest risk. In the United States, the main goal of the perpetrators was not that of killing the passengers. They hijacked the planes to attack the Twin Towers and the Pentagon, albeit absolutely mindless of the death of the innocent traveling with them. In Barbados, the basic objective of the mercenaries was to kill the passengers.

In both cases, the anguish suffered by the travelers in those final minutes of their lives, particularly the passengers on the fourth plane hijacked in the United States —who already knew what had happened in New York and Washington— must have been unbearable, the same as that of the crew and passengers of the Cuban plane during the desperate attempt to land when it was clearly impossible for them to do so. There were clear demonstrations of courage and determination in both cases as well: in Barbados, we learned of them through the recorded voices of the Cuban crew; in the United States, through subsequent reports on the attitude assumed by the passengers.

There is moving filmed footage of the horrific events in New York. As for the explosion of the plane off the coasts of Barbados and its plunge into the sea, there could not be, and there is not, so much as a photograph. The only testimony lefts are the recordings of the dramatic communications between the crew of the doomed aircraft and the Barbados airport control tower.

This was the first time in the history of Latin America that such an act had been promoted from abroad.

Actually, the systematic use of such politically motivated ruthless and fearsome practices and procedures was initiated in this hemisphere against our country. But, it was preceded in 1959 by another equally absurd and irresponsible practice: that of hijacking and diverting planes in mid-flight, a phenomenon that was practically unknown in the world at the time.

The first of such acts involved a DC-3 passenger plane bound from Havana to the Isle of Youth. It was hijacked by a few former members of Batista's tyranny repressive corps, who forced the pilot to change course and fly them to Miami. This happened on April 16, 1959, less than four months after the triumph of the Revolution. The perpetrators were never punished.

Between 1959 and 2001, a total of 51 Cuban jetliners were hijacked and most of them diverted to the United States. Many of these hijacked aircraft were never returned to our country despite the fact that not a few pilots, guards and other people were murdered or injured. Also, several planes were destroyed or seriously damaged in frustrated hijacking attempts.

The consequence of this was that the plague of "skyjacking" soon spread throughout the United States itself. For the most varied reasons, a number of individuals —the vast majority of them mentally unbalanced, thrill-seekers or common criminals, from both the United States and Latin America— started to hijack airplanes using guns, knives, Molotov cocktails, and on a number of occasions, simple bottles of water, which they claimed contained gasoline and would be used to set fire to the plane.

Thanks to the painstaking care of our authorities, not a single accident occurred upon landing. The passengers always received proper treatment and were immediately returned to their places of origin.

The majority of hijackings and diversions of Cuban aircraft took place between 1959 and 1973. Faced with the risk of a major catastrophe in the United States or Cuba —given that there were even hijackers who, once they had the plane under control, threatened to fly it into the Oak Ridge nuclear power station [in the United States] if their demands were not met— the Government of Cuba took the initiative of approaching the Government of the United States —led at the time by President Richard Nixon, with William Rogers as Secretary of State— and proposing an agreement to deal with cases of aircraft hijacking and maritime piracy. The proposal was accepted, and the agreement was quickly drawn up and signed by representatives of both governments on February 16, 1973. It was also immediately published in our country's press and given wide coverage.

That rational and well thought-out agreement established heavy sanctions against hijackers of planes and boats, and it did serve as a deterrent. From that date forward, there was a considerable reduction in the hijacking of Cuban planes, and for more than ten years, every attempted hijacking in our country was foiled.

However, the brutal terrorist attack that led to the explosion of the Cuban plane in mid-flight dealt a devastating blow to that exemplary and effective agreement. The Cuban government, faced with this inconceivable act of aggression that had taken place as part of a new wave of terrorist acts unleashed against Cuba in late 1975, denounced the agreement, in full accordance with the clauses stipulated therein. Nevertheless, it did continue to abide by the procedures set forth to prevent the hijackings of U.S. planes, including the application of heavy sanctions, which had been considerably stepped up as a result of the agreement, with sentences of up to 20 years imprisonment. Even before the agreement was signed, Cuban courts had been applying the sanctions provided in our own Penal Code against hijackers, although these had been less severe.

Despite the rigorous application of sanctions, a few other American jetliners were hijacked and diverted to our country. Then, the Government of Cuba, after issuing duly advanced warnings, decided to return two hijackers to the United States; thus, on September 18, 1980, they were delivered to the authorities of that country.

Our records show that between September 1968 and December 1984, there were 71 cases of airplanes hijacked and diverted to Cuba. Sixty-nine participants in these hijackings faced trials in courts of law and were given prison sentences ranging between three and five years. Subsequently, after the signing of the 1973 agreement, sentences ranged between 10 and 20 years.

As a result of these measures adopted by Cuba, the fact is that for the last 17 years there has not been a single further hijacking or diversion of an U.S. plane to Cuba.

On the other hand, what has been the stance of successive U.S. administrations? Since 1959, until today, the U.S. authorities have not sanctioned a single one of the hundreds of individuals who have hijacked and diverted dozens of Cuban aircraft to that country, not even those have committed murder in the course of the hijacking.

It is impossible to conceive of a greater lack of basic reciprocity, or a greater incitement to the hijacking of planes and boats. This unbending policy has remained unchanged throughout more than four decades and continues to be maintained today, without a single exception.

The constructive agreement on the hijacking of planes and boats signed between the governments of Cuba and the United States, whose results were immediately evident, was seemingly accepted by the top leaders of the terrorist groups. Some had actively cooperated or participated in the organization of irregular warfare through armed gangs that, at times, had expanded to the six former provinces of Cuba. The majority of them had been recruited by the U.S. government in the days of the Bay of Pigs invasion, the Missile Crisis, and in later years. They participated in all manner of violent actions, particularly assassination plots and terrorist attacks, that did not leave out a single sphere of the country's economic and social life, a single method, a single procedure, a single weapon.

They were taken to all kinds of institutions, schools and training programs, sometimes to be trained, sometimes to be kept busy.

Dramatic events like the assassination of President Kennedy led to in-depth investigations, like that carried out by an U.S. Senate Committee. The embarrassing situations and major scandals that resulted forced a change in tactics, although there was never really any change in the policy towards Cuba. As a consequence, after periods of relative calm, new waves of terrorism have continued to break out.

This is exactly what happened in late 1975. The Church Commission had presented its famous report on assassination plots against the leaders of Cuba and other countries on November 20 of that year, therefore, the Central Intelligence Agency could not continue assuming direct responsibility for assassination plots and terrorist acts against Cuba. The solution was simple: their most trustworthy and best-trained terrorist personnel would adopt the form of independent groups, which would act on their own behalf and under their own responsibility. This led to the sudden emergence of a bizarre coordinating organization, called the CORU, and made up by the main terrorist groups in operation, which as a rule were fiercely divided, due to leadership ambitions and personal interests. A wave of violent terrorist actions was then unleashed. To mention just a few, chosen from among the numerous and significant terrorist acts carried out during this new stage, I could point out the following that took place in a period of just four months:

- A pirate attack by speedboats from Florida against two fishing boats, leading to the death of a fisherman and serious damage to the boats, on April 6, 1976.
- A bomb planted in the Cuban embassy in Portugal, which caused the death of two diplomatic officials, serious injuries to others, and the total destruction of the premises, on April 22.
- An explosive attack against the UN Cuban Mission, causing serious material damages, on June 5.
- The explosion of a bomb on the cart carrying the luggage that was about to be loaded on a Cuba-

na Airlines flight at the Kingston, Jamaica, airport on July 9.
- The explosion of a bomb in the British West Indies Airways offices in Barbados, which represented Cubana Airlines in that country, on July 10.
- The murder of a fishing industry specialist during the attempted kidnapping of the Cuban Consul in Mérida, Mexico, on July 24.
- The abduction and vanishing of two Cuban embassy officials in Argentina, on August 9; both disappeared without a trace.
- The explosion of a bomb in the Cubana Airlines offices in Panama City, causing considerable damage, on August 18.

Obviously, this was real war. Numerous attacks were aimed at commercial airlines.

Even *The New York Times* and the *U.S. News and World Report,* two of the most prestigious publications in the United States, described it as a new wave of terrorism against Cuba.

The groups that made up the CORU, which began to operate in the first months of 1976, although it was not officially founded until June of that year, issued public statements in the United States claiming responsibility for every one of the terrorist acts they perpetrated. They sent their war dispatches —as they themselves called them— from Costa Rica to the Miami press. One of their publications printed in the moth of August an article entitled "War Dispatch" recounting the destruction of the Cuban embassy in Colombia. That was the day they did not hesitate in publishing a particularly significant communiqué signed by the five terrorist groups that made up the CORU: "Very soon we will attack airplanes in mid-flight."

To carry out their attacks, the CORU terrorists freely used as the main bases for their operations the territories of the United States, Puerto Rico, Somoza's Nicaragua, and Pinochet's Chile.

Less than eight weeks later, the Cuban jetliner would be blown up in mid-flight off the coasts of Barbados with 73 people aboard.

Hernán Ricardo and Freddy Lugo were the two Venezuelan mercenaries who planted the bomb during the Trinidad and Tobago-Barbados leg of the flight. They got off the plane in Barbados and returned to Trinidad, where they were arrested and immediately confessed to their involvement.

The Barbados police commissioner declared before an investigative committee that Ricardo and Lugo had confessed that they were working for the CIA. He added that Ricardo had pulled out a CIA card and another one where the rules for the use of C-4 plastic explosives were described.

On October 24, 1976, *The New York Times* indicated that "the terrorists who launched a wave of attacks in seven countries during the last two years were the product and instruments of the CIA."

The Washington Post noted that confirmed contacts with the U.S. embassy in Venezuela "cast doubt" on the statement issued on October 15 by U.S. Secretary of State Henry Kissinger, with regard to the claim that "no one related to the U.S. government had anything to do with the sabotage of the airplane" from Cuba.

A correspondent from the Mexican daily *Excelsior* commented from Port of Spain that "with the confession made by Hernán Ricardo Lozano, the Venezuelan detained here in Trinidad, about his responsibility in the attack on a Cubana aircraft that crashed off the coast of Barbados with 73 people aboard, a major anti-Castro terrorist network that is somehow linked with the CIA is on the verge of exposure."

Le Monde wrote that the CIA connection with Cuban-born terrorist groups that moved about freely on U.S. soil was public knowledge.

Many of the world's most respected news publications expressed the same view.

Luis Posada Carriles and Orlando Bosch, who masterminded the terrorist crime, had links with the CIA dating back to 1960. They were arrested and submitted to a dubious trial plagued with irregularities amidst enormous pressures. The Venezuelan magistrate, Dr. Delia Estaba Moreno, initiated legal proceedings against them for murder, manufacture and use of firearms, and forging and carrying of false documents. But, her honesty and integrity provoked a violent reaction among the Cuban-Venezuelan extreme right.

General Elio García Barrios, the presiding judge of the Military Appeal Court, maintained a steadfast and determined stance, thanks to which the two terrorists were forced to spend a number of years in prison. But, the Miami terrorist mob took revenge by riddling one of his sons with bullets in 1983.

Posada Carriles was rescued by the Cuban-American National Foundation, that sent 50,000 dollars via Panama to finance his escape, which was successfully carried out on August 18, 1985. In a matter of hours, he turned up in El Salvador. He was visited there, having barely arrived, by the top leaders of the Foundation. Those were the days of the dirty war in Nicaragua. He immediately began to execute important tasks under direct orders of the White House, in the air supply of weapons and explosives to the Contras in Nicaragua.

The cold figure of 73 innocent people murdered in Barbados could not possibly express the significance and magnitude of the tragedy.

Certainly, Americans will better understand by comparing the population of Cuba 25 years ago with that of the United States on September 11, 2001. The death of 73 people aboard a Cuban jetliner blown up in mid-flight is to the U.S. people as if seven American jetliners, with over 300 hundred passengers each, had been destroyed in full flight the same day, at the same time, by a terrorist conspiracy.

We could still go further and say that if we were to consider the 3,478 Cubans who have perished in over four decades as a result of acts of aggression —including the invasion by the Bay of Pigs as well as all the other terrorist acts sustained by Cuba, which originated in the United States— it would be as if 88,434 people had died in that country, that is, a figure almost similar to the number of Americans who died in the Korean and Vietnam wars combined.

This denunciation we are making here today is not inspired in either hate or rancor. I understand that American officials do not even want to hear us raise these embarrassing issues. They say that we simply should look ahead.

However, it would be senseless not to look back at the sources of errors whose repetition should be avoided, and at the causes of major human tragedies, wars and other calamities that, perhaps, could have been prevented. There should not be innocent deaths anywhere in the world.

This massive demonstration against terrorism has been called to pay homage and tribute to the memory of our brothers and sisters who died off the coasts of Barbados 25 years ago, but also to express our solidarity with the thousands of innocent people who died in New York and Washington. We are here to condemn the brutal crime committed against them while supporting the search for ways conducive to a real and lasting eradication of terrorism, to the prevalence of peace and against the development of a bloody and open-ended war.

I am deeply convinced that relations between the terrorist groups created by the United States in the first 15 years of the Revolution, to act against Cuba, and the U.S authorities have never been severed.

In a day such as this, it is only right that we ask what will be done about Posada Carriles and Orlando Bosch, the main culprits of the obnoxious terrorist act perpetrated in Barbados; and what about those who planned and financed the bombs that were set up in hotels of the country's capital and have been restlessly trying, for over four decades, to murder Cuban leaders.

It is not too much to ask that justice be done, for these professional terrorists, acting from inside the very territory of the United States, have not ceased to apply their despicable methods against our people to sow terror and to destroy the economy of a harassed and blockaded nation, one from which terrorist devices have never come —not even a gram of explosives— to blast in the United States. Never has an American been injured or killed, nor has a facility big or small in that large and rich country ever suffered the least damage from any action coming from Cuba.

As we are involved in the worldwide struggle against terrorism —committed to take part alongside the United Nations and the rest of the international community, we have the full moral authority and the right to demand the end of terrorism against Cuba. The economic warfare, itself a genocide and a brutal act to which our people have been subjected for more than 40 years, should also end.

Our brothers and sisters who died in Barbados are no longer only our martyrs, they are also symbols in the struggle against terrorism. They rise today like giants in this historic battle for the eradication of terrorism from Earth, that repulsive procedure that has caused so much damage to their home country and brought so much suffering to their closest relatives and their people that have already written unprecedented pages in the history of their Homeland and their times.

The sacrifice of their lives has not been useless. Injustice starts to shake before the eyes of a forceful and virile nation that 25 years ago cried out of indignation and sorrow, and that today cry out of emotion, of hope and pride in remembering them.

History, that can be unpredictable, has wanted it that way.

Fellow countrymen:

On behalf of the martyrs of that day in Barbados, let us say:

Socialism or Death!
Patria o muerte!
Venceremos!

Editorial: THE WAR HAS BEGUN

Yesterday, at 9:00 p.m. Afghanistan time, the war began or rather the military attack against Afghanistan. The word war suggests a conflict between more or less similar parties, where the weaker has, at least, a minimum of technical, financial and economic resources to defend itself. However, in this case, one of the parties has absolutely nothing. Still, let us call it a war. He who ordered the beginning of the military operations called it that way.

This is really a sui generis war. An entire country is being turned into a testing ground for the most sophisticated weaponry ever invented. The experts and specialists at the research centers and military workshops, who have invested tens of billions of US dollars in the creation of deadly devices, will follow attentively every detail of their creatures' performance.

Whatever the pretexts, this is a war in which the most sophisticated technology will be used against people who cannot read or write. A country whose Gross Domestic Product is 20 billion US dollars every year will be fighting another with approximately one thousand times less, therefore, for economic, cultural and religious reasons this will be a war of the old colonizers against the old colonized; of the most developed against the least developed; of the richest against the poorest; of those who call themselves civilized against those they consider ignorant and barbaric.

It is not a war against terrorism, which should and could have been defeated by truly efficient, swift and lasting means available. It is a war in favor of terrorism, since the military operations will make it more complicated and difficult to eradicate it. It is like pouring oil on the flame.

From now on, there will be a real avalanche of news about bombs, missiles, air strikes, the advance of armored vehicles with troops of ethnic groups allied with the invaders, the dropping of paratroops or the ground advance of elite forces of the attacking countries. Rather soon, there will be news about occupied cities, the capital included, and TV images of whatever censure permits or escapes control. The fight will be against the people of that country and not against the terrorists. There are no battalions or armies of terrorists. This is a sinister concept and an insidious method of struggle against a ghost.

These events will be compounded with triumphant statements, chauvinistic exaltation, boasting, braggadocio and other manifestations of arrogance and of a spirit of racial and cultural superiority.

Then, there will be the great question: Will resistance stop and every contradiction disappear or will the true war begin, that which was defined as long and open-ended? This is certainly the main question in the minds of those who are now taking pride in having launched this adventurous war.

Millions of refugees are already spreading everywhere, and the greater difficulties are still to come. Let us wait for the events to unfold.

Our people will be informed with utmost objectivity of every new occurrence, giving them more or less space in the press, radio and television depending on their importance. At the same time, we shall avoid disruptions of our everyday activities and the usual information and recreation programs.

We shall remain most attentive to the enormous efforts being made in matters related to our social and cultural development and be particularly watchful and mindful of production and services, which are today more important than ever, given all the inconveniences that the ongoing events will bring on the already deteriorated world economy whose effects no country will be able to avoid. However, no other country is better prepared and organized, and more aware than ours, to face whatever difficulties may come. Likewise, we shall continue to concentrate on our defense as we have always done.

Once again, there will be hesitation and panic in the world. Later, as the foreseeable problems begin to arise, there will be a growing awareness and a universal repudiation of the war that has just begun. Even the American people, who are today shocked by the horrible tragedy, will sooner or later understand.

Even when the opposition and condemnation of terrorism and the war, that have been the basis of our stance, —shared today by many people in the world— have sustained an expected blow with the beginning of the military operations, we shall persist struggling with all our capabilities for the only possible solution: the cessation of the military operations and the eradication of terrorism through the cooperation and support of all countries, and through the unanimous repudiation and condemnation of the international public opinion under the leadership of the United Nations Organization.

INDEX

III/ Editorial note

1/ Speech the day of the tragic events
that occurred in the United States
City of Havana, september 11, 2001

29/ Statement from the Government
of the Republic of Cuba

31/ Everything is not lost, yet

35/ Speech at the Open Forum of the Revolution
San Antonio de Los Baños,
Havana, september 22, 2001

43/ Speech at the Open Forum of the Revolution
Ciego de Ávila, september 29, 2001

51/ Declaration by the National Assembly
of People's Power of the Republic of Cuba

55/ Speech at the Open Forum of the Revolution Revolution Square, City of Havana, october 6, 2001

71/ Editorial: The war has begun